Ancient Egypt's
great pyramids are built
4,500 years ago.

Ancient China
rises to power more than
2,000 years ago.

Native American cultures
begin to thrive more than
1,500 years ago.

OUR
WORLD

NEAR & FAR

VIRGINIA

Columbus
sails to
the New
World.
1492

First
European
settlers come to
Jamestown.
1607

George
Washington
leads the
Revolutionary
War. 1776

Abraham
Lincoln writes
Emancipation
Proclamation.
1863

Susan B
Anthony
begins fight for
women's rights.
1869

Helen Keller
learns her
first words.
1886

Jackie
Robinson joins
Major League
Baseball.
1947

Martin Luther
King leads
March on
Washington.
1963

FIVE PONDS PRESS

OUR WORLD
NEAR & FAR

by Joy Masoff

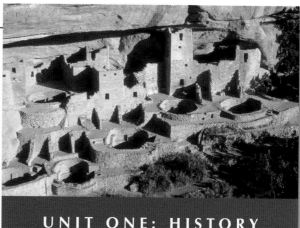

UNIT ONE: HISTORY

ADVISORY BOARD

Dr. Melissa Matusevich: Professor of Curriculum and Instruction at East Carolina University and former supervisor of Social Studies and Library Media, Montgomery County, Virginia, Public Schools.

Dr. Donald Zeigler: Professor of Geography and Political Science, Old Dominion University, Norfolk, Virginia.

REVIEWERS

Five Ponds Press wishes to acknowledge the contributions and encouragement of many Virginia public school educators. Special thanks to:
Lara Samuels of Hanover County
Kathy Morrison of Hanover County
Anita Parker of Virginia Beach
Nancy Maxwell of Fairfax County
and
Dr. Virginia Yans-McGloughlin of Rutgers University
Jason Deryck-Mahlke of John Jay High School, NY

Copyright ©2005 by Joy Masoff. All rights reserved.
Published by Five Ponds Press, Waccabuc, NY 10597.
Library of Congress Cataloging-in-Publication data available
First printing January 2005.

ISBN 0-9727156-7-3
Printed in the USA

UNIT TWO: GEOGRAPHY

UNIT FOUR: CIVICS

UNIT THREE: ECONOMICS

CHAPTER 1

OUR WORLD LONG AGO

- *Ancient people made contributions that affect the present world.*

The Forbidden City, a huge Chinese palace, is over 600 years old.

China's Great Wall extends for more than 2,100 miles. That is about the distance from Richmond, Virginia, to the California state border!

Imagine a world without TV's and computers. Picture streets without cars and homes without electric lights. No malls. No video games. Life was *very* different in **ancient** times.

But a lot of the things that we use every day came to us from long ago. At this very minute you are holding something that was invented by the people of ancient Egypt—paper! On the Fourth of July, fireworks—invented by the ancient Chinese—burst in the sky, and some of the greatest **architecture** in the world was built by these two great **civilizations** starting more than 4,000 years ago. Both places have made huge **contributions** to modern-day life.

Let us learn more about them…

Words To Know

- **Ancient**
  (AYN-shint)
  A very long time ago.

- **Architecture**
  (ark-eh-TEKT-sure)
  The design of buildings.

- **Contribution**
  (con-tri-BYOU-shun)
  The act of giving or doing something.

- **Civilization**
  (siv-uh-luh-ZAY-shun)
  A group that has a strong government as well as art, music, books, and more.

CHINA is in Asia

The Sphinx, half lion and half man, is one of the most famous structures on Earth. It guards Egypt's Pyramids.

Most of modern EGYPT is in Africa

A Pharaoh and his queen sit upon their thrones. The markings on the wall behind them are called **hieroglyphics** (Hi-row-GLIFF-iks). At first the marks were simply picture writing, but in time the pictures began to stand for sounds.

ANCIENT EGYPT

- *Many inventions of ancient Egypt are still used today.*

Ancient Egyptians called their land *Kemet*, which means "black." That is the color of the dark, rich soil that is left when the Nile River floods its banks every spring. More than 5,000 years ago one of the world's great civilizations was born here. The people who lived here were ruled by powerful kings called **pharaohs** (FAY-rows), and they did some amazing things.

The Egyptians were some of the first to develop writing. They also studied the skies and learned how to make a 365-day **calendar** that marked the Earth's trip around the sun.

Telling Time the Egyptian Way

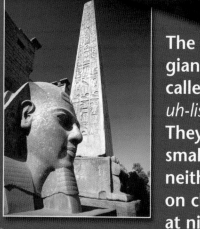

The Egyptians used giant pointy stones, called obelisks (OB-uh-liskz), as sundials. They also made smaller ones, but neither worked on cloudy days nor at night.

Water clocks worked day and night. These pots had a tiny hole at the bottom where water dripped out. They were marked with "hour" lines.

Some of the greatest gifts the ancient Egyptians left behind are the great **pyramids**. They were built as **tombs** *(toomz)* for Egypt's richest pharaohs. Deep inside each huge pyramid, the mummy of a great pharaoh was buried in a secret room filled with golden treasures. A mummy is a dead person whose body has been salted, dried, and wrapped in bandages to keep it from rotting. Today, 4,500 years after they were built, the pyramids still amaze us!

How big is each stone in the pyramids? These men are climbing on blocks that weigh 8,000 pounds a piece—about the weight of an elephant.

The Pyramids at Giza in Egypt.

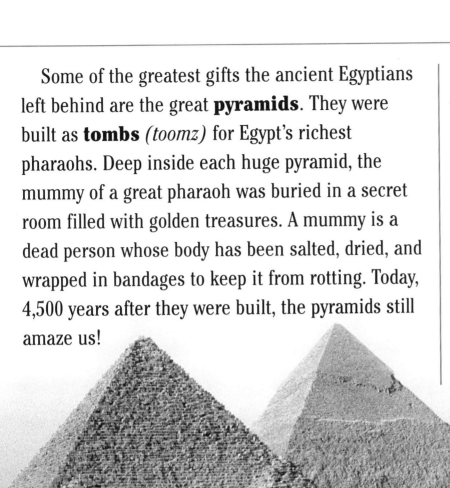

King Tut was a famous pharaoh. This gold mask was in his tomb.

Paper—Another Egyptian Contribution

A plant called papyrus *(pa-PIE-rus)* grows along the banks of the Nile. Our word "paper" comes from that word. The Egyptians made it from the fiber inside the stem of the plant. They also came up with a way of writing that became the model for the two most common alphabets in the world—Roman, the one we use, and Arabic.

7

ANCIENT CHINA

• *The people of ancient China made many contributions that are still with us today.*

Today China is the fourth largest country in the world. More people live there than in any other country on Earth. China also has one of the oldest civilizations. In this *very* big land you will find the biggest man-made structure on Earth—the Great Wall.

About 2,000 years ago a Chinese emperor decided to start building a high, thick wall to keep his enemies out. That huge wall took over 1,000 years to build!

The emperors' soldiers rounded-up more than one million people and forced them to build the wall. They worked day and night. Many died and are buried inside it!

This modern man is dressed like an ancient Chinese soldier.

Some experts say the wall was over 4,000 miles long at one time. Today it stretches over 2,100 miles—a distance as far as Virginia is to the California border, but China has given us much more than just this awesome landmark.

NEW AND IMPROVED!

About 3,500 years ago the Chinese became one of the first people to discover that when copper was heated and mixed with tin, it produced an even stronger metal called **bronze.**

Copper + Tin = Bronze

Bronze was perfect for making lovely pots and very deadly weapons. Weapons meant power.

WRITE AWAY

Like the Egyptians, the Chinese had a **written language** that used pictures. The pictures got turned into different **characters and symbols** to represent things and ideas.

日 Sun / 月 Moon = 明 Bright
This word is written by writing "sun" + "moon."

Written Chinese uses over 3,000 characters. Our alphabet uses only 26 letters. When you write, you need paper, so the Chinese figured out how to make paper from tree bark. They also made the first printing presses. They invented many wonderful things that we still use today.

Chinese Inventions

KITES were first used as weapons of war, not toys! They were used to measure distances to enemy camps.

SILK CLOTH is made by unwinding threads from silkworm cocoons after they have been put in hot water. It takes about 100 cocoons to make enough silk for a man's necktie.

A COMPASS tells you which way is north and helps you find your way. The Chinese were the first to make compasses.

FIREWORKS were another Chinese discovery. When certain chemicals are mixed together and heated, they explode. The Chinese used gunpowder to make fireworks and used both to fight wars.

CHAPTER 2

THE FIRST AMERICANS

• American Indians (First Americans) have made contributions to present-day life.

A Navajo woman watches her sheep. Sheep were used for food and their wool was used for weaving.

Different Nations with Common Bonds

ART was very important to the First Americans. They made:

BEAUTIFUL POTTERY

A Pueblo Pin

WONDERFUL WEAVINGS

JEWELRY AND BEADWORK

A Navajo Pot

A Sioux Shirt

A Navajo Rug

By the time Christopher Columbus came to America, there were already millions of people here—over 300 nations that spoke more than 140 languages! Columbus named these people "Indians" because he thought he had landed in the Indies—a group of islands in Asia. American Indians are sometimes called "First Americans" or "Native Americans" because they were living here more than 20,000 years before people from Europe started to arrive.

DARK DAYS

The American Indians suffered when the Europeans came. For one thing, the Europeans did not know it, but they carried smallpox germs. Smallpox is a deadly disease, and many American Indians got sick. Three out of every four died. Many others were forced to leave their homes and were pushed off their lands.

You are about to meet three groups of American Indians. They each had to **adapt** to the unique places where they lived, but they all helped to shape America.

America is a land of green fields, grassy plains, rocky mountains, and hot deserts. Each Indian nation had to adapt to the lands on which it lived. This Powhatan village was in Virginia.

LEGENDS AND STORIES
Tribal elders told stories about wise or wicked creatures. These stories helped children learn about life.

RESPECT FOR NATURE
The First Americans loved their lands. They took only what they needed to survive and nothing more.

RESPECT FOR THE LAND
The First Americans were good **farmers**. They understood the soil and the seasons.

This is a 400-year-old drawing of a Powhatan village. Can you guess why they built such tall fences around their homes?

Words To Know

- **Regions**

  (ree-junz)

  A group of places that have something in common. For example, the Powhatan lived in the Eastern Woodland region. The area around the Chesapeake Bay also forms a region.

VIRGINIA'S POWHATAN

- *Many American Indian tribes lived in Virginia as well as other regions of America.*

When the first explorers crossed the Atlantic from Europe and came to Virginia, they saw many things. There were thick forests, many animals, and rivers and bays bursting with fish.

They also found busy villages. Virginia had nearly 200 Powhatan settlements when colonists from England settled Jamestown in 1607. The Powhatans were part of a group we call the **Eastern Woodland Indians**.

THE RICH LAND

Woodlands are **regions** with lots of trees. The dense forests gave the Powhatans almost everything they needed to live well—turkeys, rabbits, squirrels, deer, and bear. There was bark and wood for building houses and canoes. Life was very good for the Powhatans.

The lands of the Eastern Woodland Indians

The Powhatan men used every last bit of a hunted animal. Powhatans ate the meat and used the bones to make tools. They took the sinew (the part that holds muscle to bone) and used it for sewing and making strings for their bows. They used the skins from deer, bear, and other animals to make clothing.

POWHATAN PRIDE

Women did most of the farming. They taught their kids how to plant and harvest roots, nuts, and fruit. The women cooked over outdoor fire pits and stirred up yummy stews. They ground corn to bake tasty breads and smoked meats and fish, which they stored in baskets to eat during the winter when food was scarce.

For many hundreds of years, the Powhatan lived happily along Virginia's rivers and bays, until the arrival of explorers and settlers from Europe ended their way of life.

The Powhatan grew corn, beans, and squash. Women did most of the farming while the men hunted and fished.

They got around on foot or by canoe. They wore soft leather shoes called moccasins.

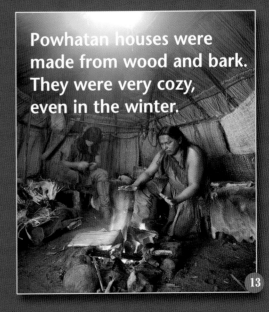

Powhatan houses were made from wood and bark. They were very cozy, even in the winter.

Plains Indians moved a lot. They lived in easy-to-move teepees made of animal hides. In winter the teepees were lined with fur for extra warmth.

Plains Indians were amazing **hunters**. Having horses helped make herding buffalo easier.

There were other Plains Indians such as the Cheyenne, Crow, and Comanche.

Sacagawea (Sock-uh-guh-WEE-uh), is famous for helping Lewis and Clark as they explored America's West. She has been honored with a gold-colored $1 coin.

PEOPLE OF
THE PLAINS

- *American Indians (First Americans) met their basic needs in different ways.*

The land of the Plains Indians was *very* different from the Powhatans' lands. Their lives were different too. They did not farm much. Instead, they lived by hunting.

Plains are flat areas with very few hills or trees. They are often covered by grasses—both tall and short. Grasses are perfect for grazing animals, and the grains from the grasses are used to make bread. Just 200 years ago the lands between the Mississippi River and the Rocky Mountains were home to more than 150,000 American Indians and 60 *million* buffalo.

THE BUFFALO HUNTERS

The **Sioux** *(SOO)* were the biggest group of Plains Indians. They survived by hunting. Because there were no horses in America until Spanish explorers brought them here in the 1500's, the Plains Indians first hunted on foot. They herded the buffalo over cliffs or into deep pits, then shot the trapped animals with arrows.

Sitting Bull was a famous Sioux leader.

The lands of the Plains Indians.

When the Plains Indians saw their first horses, they called them "sacred dogs." They quickly learned about these new creatures and became the best riders in America. Horses made their lives so much easier.

FIGHTING MAD

Unlike the Eastern Woodlands Indians (who *tried* to get along), the Plains Indians fought a lot with each other. They were great warriors because the same skills that helped them kill huge buffalos—no fear and great skill with bows and arrows—served them well when fighting their human enemies.

When the United States government tried to push the Plains Indians off their lands, they fought back. They won a famous battle at a place called Little Big Horn, but they were no match for the soldiers' guns and cannons. By the late 1800's, the last of the Plains Indians were forced onto reservations. They could no longer hunt for buffalo. It was a very sad time for them.

Today some Plains Indians still live on reservations.

These Sioux warriors were hunting buffalo. They used the meat for food, the skins for clothes and tepees, the bones to make tools, and the tendons to make thread and bow-strings. They boiled the hoofs to make glue and made arrow shafts from the ribs. Nothing went to waste!

Words To Know

- **Reservations**
  (rez-ur-VAY-shunz)
  Land that American Indians were forced to move to after being pushed away from their homes.

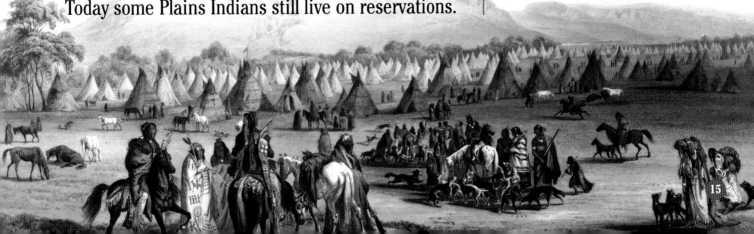

THE LAND OF THE PUEBLO

- *Life in America's Southwest was very different from the Plains and the Woodlands.*

The Southwest is a land of deep canyons, cactus-filled deserts, and the **Pueblo Indians**. The Navajo, Zuni, and Hopi are some of the Pueblo peoples. Pueblo is a Spanish word that means "village."

It is very dry in the Southwest, and it can get really hot, yet nights in the desert can be freezing. The Pueblo peoples built houses with very thick walls made from *adobe (uh-DOE-bee)*—sun-dried bricks made of clay and straw. Their *adobe* homes kept them warm at night and cool during the hottest days.

Pueblo people are famous for their jewelry, pots, and colorful weavings. Moms still teach their daughters how to make all sorts of beautiful crafts.

The Village People

Pueblo women learned to spin the wool from the sheep they raised to make yarn for rugs.

This Pueblo town has multi-story terraced buildings. Terraces are large, flat areas. People still build their homes this way in parts of the Southwest.

This is Mesa Verde, in Colorado. The Pueblo Indians lived in this area for more than 800 years.

Why do you think they built their houses under this big rock?

PUEBLO LIFE

The Pueblo Indians grew squash, beans, and corn using very little water. They hunted rabbit and raised sheep for food and wool.

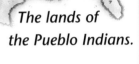

The lands of the Pueblo Indians.

Some Pueblo peoples lived in cities, but those cities were quite different from the cities of today. Chaco Canyon was one of the biggest Pueblo cities. It was built 1,100 years ago. One building alone had over 700 apartments and special round rooms, called kivas, where people gathered for religious ceremonies.

The Pueblo Indians were very different from the Sioux or the Powhatan, but they had one sad thing in common. They too were forced from their homes by settlers from Europe, yet even though they lost their land, they have kept their ancient ways alive.

These are the ruins of Chaco Canyon. The round rooms are the kivas (KEE-vuhz). Everyone left the city in 1250, but no one knows why.

The Pueblo people have always had great faith in the spirit world. They use kachinas—spirit-dolls—to teach children right from wrong. There are kachinas for the spirits of the rain, sun, wind, and many others.

CHAPTER 3

A WORLD OF CHANGE

• *Communities change over time for a variety of reasons.*

The first cars had no windows or roofs. Roads were bumpy. Today giant superhighways connect the entire country. What a change!

The way people live today is very different from the way people lived 100 years ago. Back then there were no radios or TV's. There were no electric lights, airports, six-lane highways, or skyscrapers. Refrigerators had not been invented to keep food cold, and a trip from Virginia to California took weeks and weeks.

But suddenly things started to change—slowly at first, then faster and faster.

A Changing Richmond, Then...

This is what Richmond, Virginia looked like in 1863 at the time of the Civil War.

NEW INVENTIONS

Between 1890 and 1930, people saw many changes. Light bulbs began to light up houses. Airplanes flew through the clouds. New ways of building made skyscrapers possible, and elevators made getting to the top much easier. Many folks went from working on farms to working in factories, from living in log cabins to living in apartment buildings, and from riding horses to driving cars.

In the 1930's a lot of skyscrapers—very tall buildings—were built. This work crew eats lunch on a steel beam of the Empire State Building in New York.

NEW JOBS

All these new inventions meant that people had to learn new skills. Car factories needed people to put the cars together. Airplanes needed pilots to fly them. Skyscrapers needed construction workers to build them and office workers to use them. America quickly changed from a nation of farmers and shopkeepers to a land where people could choose from thousands of different jobs. Many of these new jobs were in cities.

Words To Know

- **Community**
  (Com-MEW-nit-ee)
  A place where people live, work, and play.

- **Population**
  (POP-u-lay-shun)
  The number of people living in a community.

- **Transportation**
  (trans-port-A-shun)
  A way of moving people and things from one place to another.

...and Now

The James River still runs through Richmond today, but the city has changed a lot. What are some of the ways it is different? How is it still the same?

CHANGING COMMUNITIES

- *How have communities changed over time?*

Communities change as people move around more. Folks can now do that easily because we now have good **transportation**—trains, cars, and planes to move us from one place to another. **Populations** also change. With better transportation, people left the country and moved to the cities where there were chances to find good jobs. People could even move to places on the other side of the country. These charts and graphs will tell you more about those changes.

WHAT IS THE FASTEST WAY TO GO?

It is 340 miles from New York City to Richmond. Long ago the only way to make the trip was by foot or on horseback. Today you can get there very quickly. Which is the fastest way to go?

WALK about 13 days

HORSE about 8½ days

| 13 Days |
| 12 Days |
| 11 Days |
| 10 Days |
| 9 Days |
| 8 Days |
| 7 Days |
| 6 Days |
| 5 Days |
| 4 Days |
| 3 Days |
| 2 Days |
| 1 Day |

TRAIN about 7 hours

CAR about 6 hours

JET less than 2 hours

HOW HAS VIRGINIA'S POPULATION CHANGED?

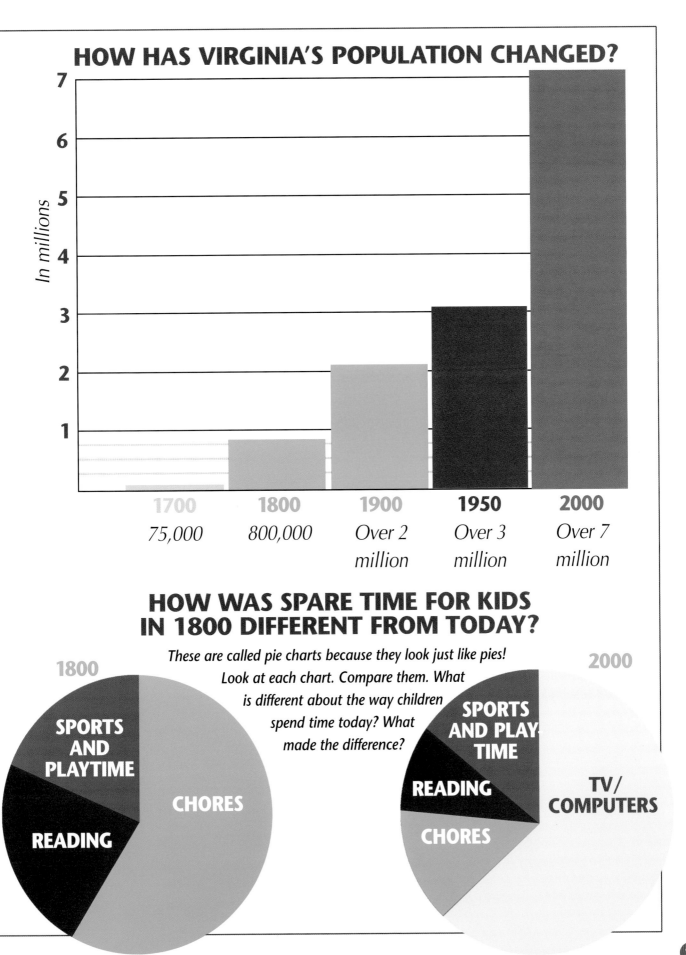

In millions

1700	1800	1900	1950	2000
75,000	800,000	Over 2 million	Over 3 million	Over 7 million

HOW WAS SPARE TIME FOR KIDS IN 1800 DIFFERENT FROM TODAY?

These are called pie charts because they look just like pies! Look at each chart. Compare them. What is different about the way children spend time today? What made the difference?

1800

SPORTS AND PLAYTIME

CHORES

READING

2000

SPORTS AND PLAYTIME

READING

CHORES

TV/ COMPUTERS

21

CHAPTER 4

LIVING IN OUR WORLD

• *People adapt to their environment in many different ways.*

Words To Know

• **Geography**

(gee-OGG-ruh-fee)
The study of our environment and how it affects us.

We have learned about five great civilizations. Each was very different, but one of the biggest ways they differ is the **geography** of each place. Some of Earth's places are hot and dry. Others are cool and rainy. Some have cold winters. Others have *no* winters. Some have mountains. Others are flat. The people of each place had to **adapt**—find ways to survive—in the lands where they were born.

Chinese farmers changed their environment by cutting terraces—flat areas—into the side of this mountain.

It is very rainy here, so it is perfect for growing rice.

A World of Difference

Egypt's long river, the Nile, used to flood its banks every spring, leaving rich soil for planting. It was also a good way to travel from city to city.

America's Great Plains have miles of grassland. Grasses are good for grazing animals like cows and buffalo.

China has mountains, rivers, and valleys. Its varied climate allowed people to grow a lot of wheat in the north and rice in the south.

Long ago, people learned to make the desert bloom. They figured out a way to grow crops on the sides of steep mountains. They dug out tree trunks to make boats. People in each region did things a little differently, but people everywhere learned to *use* their **environment** and sometimes even *change* it. Let's find out more…

Words To Know

- **Climate**
  (KLI-mit)
  The kind of weather an area has over a long period of time.

- **Land**
  The shape of the Earth's surface.

- **Environment**
  (En-VY-run-ment)
  All the things around you.

WAYS TO
SURVIVE

- *People adapt to their environment in different ways.*

These Chinese women are picking rice. Rice is a type of grain that comes from a grass that grows in very wet areas. What American Indian group depended on other kinds of grains to survive?

ANCIENT CHINA

The Chinese **fished** and **farmed**. They did much of their fishing at night by using lanterns, which attract the fish to the surface. They also cut terraces into their hills to make flat areas on which to plant. Those flat areas helped **irrigate** the crops by trapping rainwater.

ANCIENT EGYPT

The ancient Egyptians **irrigated** and **farmed** the land near the Nile River. They dug canals from the river, dragging rocks through the mud. Today farmers still use the old ways. These children are riding on a rock being dragged to make a furrow.

The lands on which we live give us many gifts—food to eat, trees with which to build houses, and water to drink. Every land has its own special mix of things. Some places are too dry while others are too cold. Sometimes it is not easy to survive. People have learned how to use the land on which they live.

Words To Know
- **Irrigate**
  (EAR-uh-gate)
  To bring water for crops from somewhere else.

THE POWHATAN

The Powhatans **farmed, fished,** and **hunted**. They **used trees** to build homes and canoes, and they **gathered** and **grew plants** for food. This is a drawing of a Powhatan fishing at night. He was about to spear a fish using torchlight, just like the Chinese fishers.

THE SIOUX

The Sioux were always moving to **hunt buffalo**. Before Europeans brought horses to the Americas, the Sioux hunted on foot. Horses made their lives easier. The grasses of the plains fed the horses, and the grains from the grasses were ground to make bread.

THE PUEBLO

The Pueblo **farmers** knew how to grow crops using very little water. They also raised sheep. They lived in **villages** in **adobe** houses. Adobe is made by mixing clay soil with straw and then baking the mixture into blocks in the hot desert sun.

HOW'S THE CLIMATE?

• *Different lands have different climates.*

Every morning when you wake up, you probably look out the window. Is it sunny or raining or snowing? Is it hot or cold? Humid or dry? Windy or still? Every day people look out windows or go outside to check the weather.

HOT DRY DAYS

Water is scarce in the land of the **Pueblo**. Nights can be very cold.

ICY COLD WINTERS

Winters in **the Plains** are freezing. Summers are the opposite— really hot!

WARM ALL YEAR

Egypt's weather is the same most of the year —hot and dry.

FOUR SEASONS

Parts of **China**, like **Virginia**, have four different seasons with warm summers and cool winters.

To find out what will happen later in the day or week, folks look in a newspaper or watch a weather person on TV. The kind of weather a region has over a long period of time is called its **climate**. **Virginia** has four seasons with mild winters and hot, humid summers. That is *our* climate. **Egypt** has a hot, dry climate with very little rain.

VERY DIFFERENT CLIMATES

Ancient people learned to understand their climate—to know when to plant, when to harvest, and when to bundle up and stay inside.

The Powhatan had mild winters and hot, humid summers. That kind of climate helps trees grow, so there were thick woodlands. Crops also grew well in this wet climate.

The Plains Indians had to deal with harsher weather. Hot summers brought thunderstorms and tornados. Winters meant bone-chilling cold and heavy snows. Growing crops was much harder here.

The Pueblo people lived in places where temperatures could reach 115 degrees Farenheit during the summer. Long periods without rain made it hard to grow crops. Nights in the desert can be cold, so the Pueblo needed houses that stayed cool during the day and warm at night.

The people in each group learned to adapt to their climate and found ways to make life as comfy as possible.

Going to Extremes

Sometimes the weather turns scary. Certain parts of the world can get hit by some really wild weather.

The Plains Indians had to deal with tornados. A tornado is a swirling funnel of air. It is the worst kind of storm on Earth. Winds in the center of the funnel can reach 300 miles per hour!

Both **Virginia** and **China** can be hit by hurricanes—storms with winds that top 74 miles per hour. In China, hurricanes are called typhoons. Hurricanes form over the ocean, so places on the coast often get hit the hardest.

GROWING SEASONS

- *How are the climate, land, and plant life of China, Egypt, and the regions of the Powhatan, Sioux, and Pueblo similar and different?*

Our planet has places where it is so hot you can fry an egg on a rock. In Antarctica the temperature can drop to 120 degrees below zero Farenheit. The Earth's surface rises up over five miles high at the top of its tallest mountain, Everest, in Asia. It dips down almost seven miles deep in the South Pacific Ocean. From hot to cold, high to low—we live in a world of contrasts.

OUR DIVERSE PLANET

You might not think that China, Egypt, and America's Southwest would have something big in common, but they do. Can you tell what it is? How is Virginia different from the Great Plains? This chart will help you compare these five regions.

EGYPT

CHINA

EASTERN WOODLANDS
(Powhatan)

PLAINS
(Sioux)

SOUTHWEST
(Pueblo)

CLIMATE	LAND	PLANTS
• It is very **hot** and **dry** in Egypt. It rains only about 3 times a year.	• The **Nile River** cuts through the **desert**. It used to **flood** every summer.	• **Tall grasses** such as papyrus grow along the Nile. Almost nothing grows in the desert.
• Much of China has **four seasons**, like Virginia. China also has the Gobi **desert,** one of the Earth's driest.	• China has it all— **forests, hills, mountains**, and its great **desert**, the Gobi.	• China has a **great variety of plant life**— more than 32,000 kinds!
• Virginia has **mild winters** and **hot, humid summers**. It rains more than 40 inches a year.	• The woodlands have **rivers, forests, hills,** and **mountains.** Its **coastal plain** hugs the Atlantic Ocean.	• Trees, bushes, vines, grasses, and a **wide variety of plant life** grow in the Eastern Woodlands.
• The Great Plains have **harsh, cold winters** and **hot summers**. Winter temperatures can reach 60° F. below zero.	• Miles of **rolling hills** meet flat areas of **plains** on the vast **prairie** in the middle of America.	• The Plains' **grasslands** are called America's bread basket because tons of wheat grow there.
• The Southwest can have very **hot days**, yet **cold nights** are common. It rains only about 14 inches a year.	• **High flatlands**, called *mesas,* rise up from scrubby **deserts**. "Mesa" means table in Spanish.	• **Cacti**— some more than 40 feet tall— dot the desert.

CHAPTER 5

WHERE IN THE WORLD?

- *Maps and globes help people study the Earth.*
- *Maps can be used to locate land—places where people live—and water features.*

NORTH AMERICA

ATLANTIC OCEAN

PACIFIC OCEAN

EQUATOR

Words To Know

- **Equator**
  (e-KWAY-tur)
  An imaginary line around the middle of the Earth.

- **Continent**
  (CON-tin-ent)
  A large body of land on the Earth.

SOUTH AMERICA

ATLANTIC OCEAN

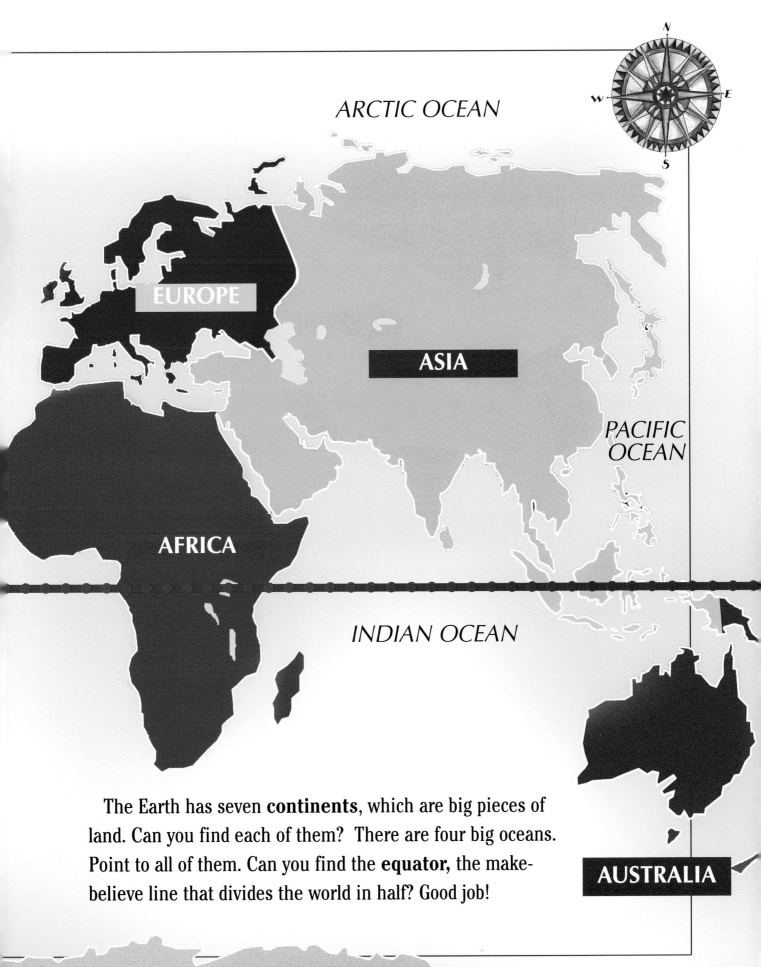

ARCTIC OCEAN

EUROPE

ASIA

PACIFIC OCEAN

AFRICA

INDIAN OCEAN

AUSTRALIA

The Earth has seven **continents**, which are big pieces of land. Can you find each of them? There are four big oceans. Point to all of them. Can you find the **equator,** the make-believe line that divides the world in half? Good job!

ANTARCTICA

• *Where are the major rivers, lakes, and mountain ranges located on the map of the United States?*

MAPPING

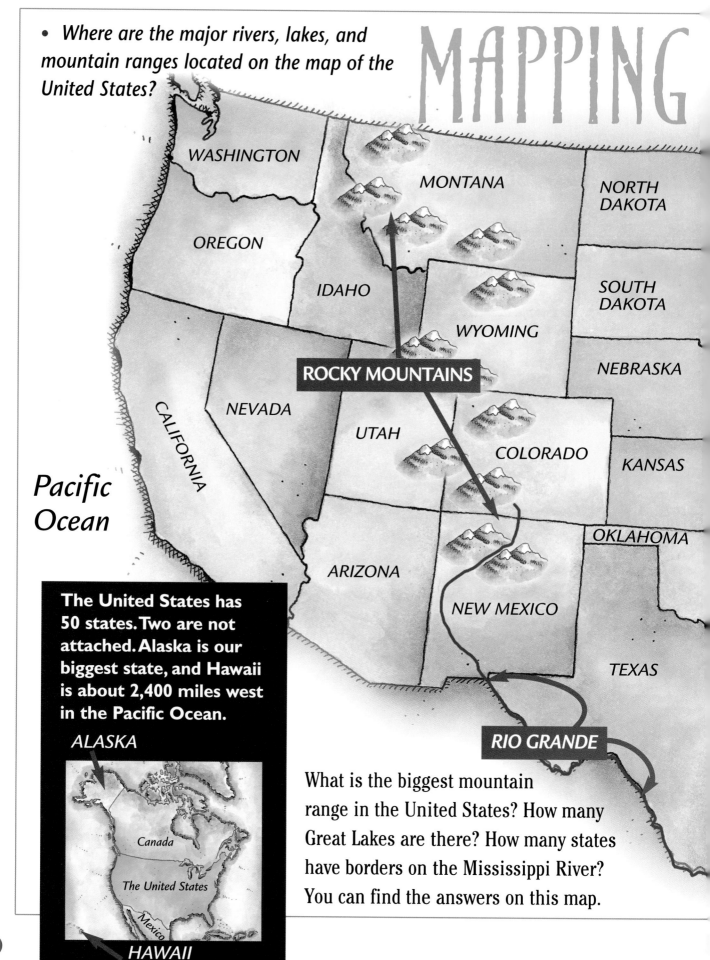

WASHINGTON

MONTANA

NORTH DAKOTA

OREGON

IDAHO

SOUTH DAKOTA

WYOMING

ROCKY MOUNTAINS

NEBRASKA

Pacific Ocean

NEVADA

CALIFORNIA

UTAH

COLORADO

KANSAS

OKLAHOMA

ARIZONA

NEW MEXICO

TEXAS

The United States has 50 states. Two are not attached. Alaska is our biggest state, and Hawaii is about 2,400 miles west in the Pacific Ocean.

ALASKA

Canada

The United States

Mexico

HAWAII

RIO GRANDE

What is the biggest mountain range in the United States? How many Great Lakes are there? How many states have borders on the Mississippi River? You can find the answers on this map.

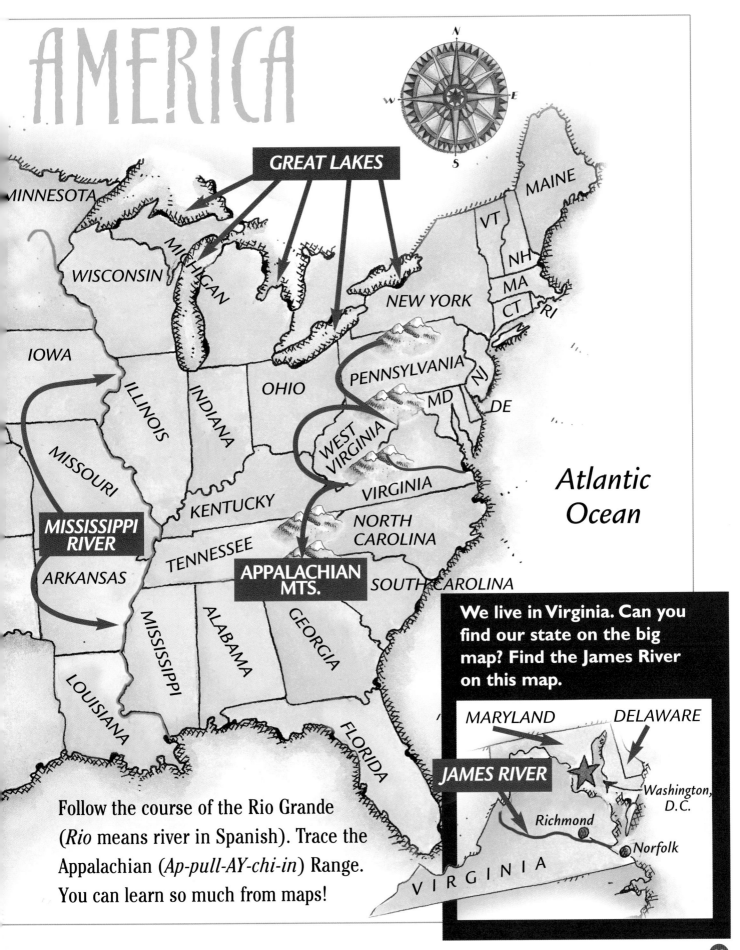

AMERICA

GREAT LAKES

MINNESOTA

WISCONSIN

MICHIGAN

IOWA

ILLINOIS

INDIANA

OHIO

MISSOURI

MISSISSIPPI RIVER

KENTUCKY

ARKANSAS

TENNESSEE

MISSISSIPPI

ALABAMA

GEORGIA

LOUISIANA

PENNSYLVANIA

WEST VIRGINIA

VIRGINIA

NORTH CAROLINA

APPALACHIAN MTS.

SOUTH CAROLINA

MAINE

VT

NH

MA

CT

RI

NEW YORK

NJ

MD

DE

Atlantic Ocean

FLORIDA

Follow the course of the Rio Grande (*Rio* means river in Spanish). Trace the Appalachian (*Ap-pull-AY-chi-in*) Range. You can learn so much from maps!

We live in Virginia. Can you find our state on the big map? Find the James River on this map.

MARYLAND

DELAWARE

JAMES RIVER

Washington, D.C.

Richmond

Norfolk

VIRGINIA

CHAPTER 6

MAKING MAPS

- *A map is a drawing that shows what places look like from above and where these places are located.*

- *Maps include a title, map legend, and compass rose.*

- *A map legend includes symbols that represent objects and places.*

From up in space, the world is a big blue, green, and white ball. You can barely see the continents, let alone a roadway! People need help finding places. The easiest way to discover how to get from one place to another is to use a map. A map shows a bird's-eye view of what a place looks like and where it is located.

Long ago, people drew maps from their memories of seeing a place. Explorers made notes as they sailed or walked across strange, new lands. Kings used hand-drawn maps to keep track of all the lands they owned.

Today it is so much easier. Satellites up in space take amazing pictures of our Earth.

Pictures from the Sky

Modern map makers take photos of the Earth from airplanes or satellites.

This satellite photo shows parts of Portsmouth and Norfolk, Virginia. Look closely and you will be able to see bridges, docks, houses, and even boats on the water.

THE PARTS OF A MAP

A COMPASS ROSE is a symbol on a map that points north, south east, and west.

A MAP TITLE tells you what the map shows.

MAP OF VIRGINIA

A MAP LEGEND lists symbols and their meanings.

A MAP SCALE tells you how big the land really is so you know how far apart things are.

Drawings of the Land

Compare this map with the one on the left. Can you match the water parts and bridges? Can you see the highways? A map maker has used the satellite photo to draw all the important parts.

Map makers have marked the roads and parks. They have put names on the streets and rivers. It is easy to find places now!

CHAPTER 7

This man is cutting down a tree with a chain saw. What is the natural resource? The capital resource? The human resource?

OUR USEFUL
WORLD

The three main types of resources are natural, human, and capital.

water **soil**

wood **coal**

NATURAL RESOURCES
Things that come directly from the Earth

soldier **miner** **builder** **doctor**

HUMAN RESOURCES
People at work, making things, or helping others

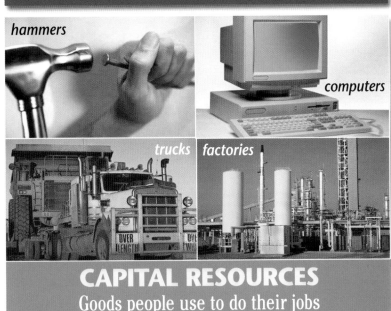

hammers

computers

trucks **factories**

CAPITAL RESOURCES
Goods people use to do their jobs

Humans are very creative. We have looked at nature's gifts, our **natural resources,** and put them to work.

We can take a tree and find dozens of different ways to use it. We build houses from the lumber and make paper by mashing up the pulp. Sap from maple trees gives us syrup. Rubber comes from the sap of rubber trees. Aspirin is made with a powder from the bark of the willow. That is just a start!

Can you look at the pictures on this page and think of other **natural, human,** and **capital resources**?

Words To Know

- **Natural resources**
Materials that come from nature.

- **Human resources**
People working to produce goods and services.

- **Capital resources**
Goods made by people and used to produce other goods and services.

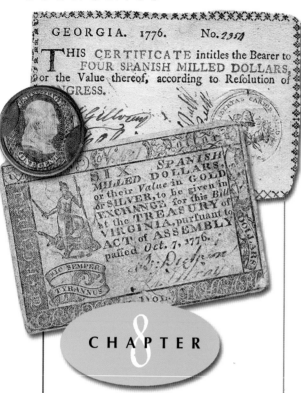

Back when America was a very new country, every state had its own money. These very old bills are from Georgia and Virginia. People even used postage stamps stuck on bits of metal as money.

CHAPTER 8

THE STORY OF MONEY

• *People get goods and services through barter or by exchanging money.*

If a person fixes the family car or cuts your hair, he or she has done a **service** for you. When you go to a store, the things you buy—from TV's to shoes—are sometimes called **goods**. In both cases, getting that haircut or shopping for new sneakers is going to cost you **money**!

For thousands of years, there was no such thing as money. There were no stores and nothing to buy. People hunted to survive, so they were always on the move. They made everything they needed to live.

Salt slabs, worth as much as gold in parts of Africa, were one of the first types of money.

Wampum was made from very special shells and was worn as a belt. It was used by both colonists and American Indians.

Native Americans traded furs as well as wampum for metal pots, knives, and cloth.

As people settled down, things changed. They now had a little extra time to do other things. They wove cloth and made pots. Some folks were really good at these things, so other villagers had time to trade, or **barter**, their extra corn for a pretty belt or swap an animal skin for a bowl.

SMALL CHANGE

About 3,000 years ago in the Middle East, the Sumerians melted silver into small equal-sized bars. They were easier to carry around than a cow or 20 pounds of grain, and they could be used to buy both! The first money had been invented. Small and easy to carry, it stood for something of value. Gold, which was very rare, soon became one of the things that was used for money. People broke off bits of their gold to pay for things. Coins were born!

About 1,000 years ago the Chinese started to use paper money. The idea soon spread to Europe and finally to America.

Words To Know

- **Barter**
(BAR-tur)
The exchange of goods and services without the use of money. You might, for example, wash your neighbor's car in exchange for an ice cream cone.

- **Money**
Coins and paper bills used in exchange for goods and services. Paying for a load of lumber with ten goats is messy. Paying with money is easy.

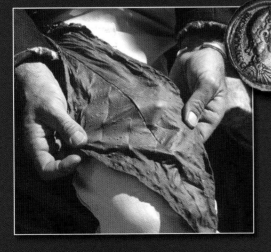

Tobacco, which was sometimes called "country pay," was used as money in Virginia for 200 years.

Gold and silver were used to make coins all over the world. Gold is rare and very valuable.

Today banks issue credit and debit cards. People pay the bank to use these cards.

CHAPTER 9

Every day we make decisions about what we are going to buy. This boy wants to buy lots of cookies. Do you think his mother will let him?

Words To Know

- **Consumer**
  (con-SOO-mur)
  A person who uses goods and services.

- **Producer**
  (pro-DOO-sir)
  A person who uses resources to make goods, or a person who provides services.

- **Scarcity**
  (SCARE-sa-tee)
  Not being able to meet all wants at the same time.

BUYING AND SELLING

- *People are both producers and consumers.*

- *People must make economic choices because resources are limited (scarcity).*

Having a lemonade stand is fun. Start with some **natural resources**—lemons and sugar. Add in some **capital resources**—tables, pitchers, and cups. Don't forget the most important part—**human resources**—to make and sell drinks!

Take a closer look at the lemonade stand. The kids who run the stand are all **consumers** because they had to buy lemons, sugar, cups, and pitchers. They needed paper, paint, and tape to make signs for their business. They are also **producers**. They have taken raw "goods" and put them together to make something new. They have "produced" some tasty lemonade!

ALL GONE

Sometimes companies run out of the things they are making, or there are not enough people around to do a particular job. When that happens, there is a **scarcity**. This often occurs around the holidays when certain toys become really popular. Sometimes you have to wait months for the factory to make more of that toy.

From time to time, there are not enough people to do certain jobs. In some places there is a scarcity of doctors, teachers, or nurses. Being really sick with no doctor to help is a *scary* scarcity. Not having enough teachers means that classes will have too many students. We often have to make tough choices because resources, goods, and services are limited.

Producers need consumers to buy their products. Consumers need producers to make the things they need. It is that simple!

Making an Economic Choice

Something sweet? Something fun? What would you choose?

You could buy two ice cream cones...OR

...you could buy a toy ...OR

WHAT WOULD YOU DO WITH $5.00?

...you could go to the movies ...OR

...you could save the money and buy something bigger later...OR

...you could give the money to charity and help others. What would you do?

41

What Makes You a Good Citizen?

You can do things that will improve your school and community.

You can help make decisions by voting "yes" or "no" on important classroom issues.

Showing self-reliance, self-discipline, and always helping others will make you an A+ citizen!

CHAPTER 10

MAKING A BETTER WORLD

- *A good citizen has a variety of responsibilities.*

Have you ever had a run-in with a school bully? Have you ever seen someone cheating on a test? Have you ever stepped in a puddle of milk in the cafeteria that someone did not clean up? Those children are not being very nice!

Your classroom is a good place to start thinking about what makes a good citizen.

Don't cheat! Cheating only hurts the cheater!

DOING THE RIGHT THING

When you get to school in the morning, do you push getting off the bus? On the playground do you boss others around and grab things? A good citizen always respects other people's rights and property. That means asking if you may borrow a pencil or a crayon. It means following the rules. It means treating people the way you would like them to treat you.

Don't grab! Play fair! Follow the rules.

TANTRUMS? OH NO!

Yelling out answers without raising a hand or pushing someone out of the lunch line are signs that a child does not have **self-discipline**. Tantrums will never get anyone anywhere. Good citizens can control themselves even when they are bursting to share the right answer or want to get the first helping of macaroni and cheese.

People who are **self-reliant** get things done without having to be reminded. Doing homework or taking care of your pets without being nagged makes you a good citizen. Always telling the truth and being **trustworthy**—being the kind of person others feel they can turn to when they need help—will make you a good citizen and a GREAT friend!

Words To Know

- **Self-discipline**
  (SELF DISS-uh-plin)
  Being able to control your impulses and urges.

- **Self-reliance**
  (SELF ree-LIE-ins)
  Being able to do things by yourself.

- **Trustworthiness**
  (TRUST-wur-thee-nes)
  Making people feel that they can depend on you to do a good job.

GREAT AMERICANS

Meet some of the people in America's past who worked very hard to make life better.

GEORGE WASHINGTON

- *He led the fight for freedom from England and helped establish a new country.*

Without George Washington there might not be a United States. He did so many things!

After America declared its independence from England in 1776, Washington was asked to lead the new army. Like many others, Washington had served in the British* army fighting the French years before. He had led Virginia's soldiers in that war, so he knew how the British fought. This came in handy when it was time to fight *against* England.

England, along with Scotland, Northern Ireland, and Wales, are all parts of Great Britain. People who live in England can be called either English or British.

The Washington Monument is the tallest building in our nation's capital—Washington, D.C. How does it compare to the obelisk on page 6?

From Farmer to Soldier to President

Washington was born in Virginia in 1732. When he was 11, his father died, so he moved to his half-brother's farm, Mount Vernon.

Washington's first job was making maps for Virginia's Lord Fairfax, but he wanted some excitement. In 1753 he joined the Virginia militia *(ma-lish-uh)* and learned how to be a soldier. By 1755 Washington was leading the *entire* Virginia militia.

Washington was elected to the House of Burgesses *(BURR-jis-iz)* in 1758. They were the people who made laws for Virginia. Washington heard Patrick Henry speak out against the British.

READY, AIM, FIRE!

In the first years of the Revolutionary War, the new army kept losing. Washington knew he had to try something different. He took risks. He fought at night and in bad weather. In 1778 he spent a terrible winter at Valley Forge, Pennsylvania, training his troops. His hard work started to pay off. His soldiers started winning.

Washington surprised the enemy by crossing the icy Delaware River on Christmas Eve in 1776.

In October 1781, after six years of war, the British gave up. America was free at last! A very tired Washington came home to his farm at Mount Vernon, but the new nation needed him for an even bigger job and elected him as America's first President—the person who would lead the new nation.

FATHER OF OUR COUNTRY

On April 30, 1789, George Washington took the very first Oath of Office. Going first meant he had to figure out how to do just about everything, but, as he did everything in life, he did it well.

Five years after the war ended, Washington was needed again. In 1787 he went to Philadelphia to help write the Constitution— a plan of government for our country. In 1789 Washington was elected President. He was re-elected in 1792 and led America for a total of 8 years.

WASHINGTON 3 2002
333-MDE
EVERGREEN STATE

Washington is the only President to have a state named after him. Our nation's capital is named after him too. Virginia has a Washington County and so do 29 other states!

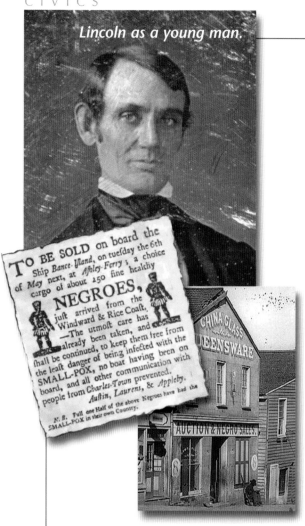

Lincoln as a young man.

Can you believe that people used to be bought and sold? This slave auction house was in Atlanta, Georgia. Young Abe Lincoln hated the idea of slavery.

Words To Know

• **Emancipate**
(ih-MAN-sih-payt)
To free someone from slavery.

ABRAHAM
LINCOLN

• **He was the President of the United States who helped free African American slaves.**

Our country is called the *United* States of America, but in the 1860's, something happened to rip our country apart. As people moved west, our country grew bigger. New states joined the Union (the states that made up our nation). Would slavery be allowed in these states? People in the South said "yes." Folks in the North said "no." That argument led to a terrible war—the Civil War.

HONEST ABE

Abraham Lincoln was America's President during this awful time. Lincoln was the kind of person people liked—honest, gentle, and funny. He was born in a log cabin in Kentucky in 1809. Lincoln loved books, and he read all the time. He also split rails, worked as a farmer, owned a grocery store, was a captain in a volunteer army, became a lawyer, served as a judge, and then ran for political office.

At first he lost quite a few elections, but Lincoln was a fine speaker, and he finally won an important election. He became our 16th President in 1861.

A COUNTRY DIVIDED

Lincoln had promised to try to keep the Union together. When he became President, the eleven southern states that wanted to keep their slaves broke away from the United States. They created a new country and called it the *Confederate States of America*. Like a family torn apart by divorce, America was no longer *united*. Lincoln had no choice but to go to war to re-unite America.

FREE AT LAST

On January 1, 1863, Lincoln wrote the **Emancipation** *(ee-man-suh-PAY-shun)* **Proclamation** *(prock-luh-MAY-shun)*, which freed the slaves in all the rebel southern states. When they heard they were free, many former slaves in the South joined the Union Army and helped the North win the war.

On April 9, 1865, Robert E. Lee, the head of the Confederate Army, gave up the fight. The war was over, and the states were united once again. Lincoln looked forward to mending his broken country, but that was not to be.

Five days later Lincoln was shot and killed as he watched a play in Washington, D.C. Today he is still remembered and honored as one of America's greatest heroes.

The Lincoln Memorial is in our nation's capital.

From Sadness to Joy

Free States
Border States
Slave states that left the Union before the Civil War began
Slave states that left the Union after the Civil War began

There were three types of states. **Free states** had no slavery. **Slave states** did. **Border states** had slaves, but they did not leave the Union. Virginia was a slave state.

Lincoln freed the slaves in all the slave states. The people who were now free were so happy!

What is **Juneteenth**? On June 19, 1865, slaves in Texas learned that they were free. They celebrated with big parties. This very happy holiday soon spread to the rest of the South.

Best friends, Susan B. Anthony (standing) and Elizabeth Cady Stanton (sitting), spent more than 40 years working to win the vote for women.

MEN, who love the Freedom which your Fathers won for You, Pay your Debt by Winning Freedom for your Daughters.

VOTES FOR WOMEN

Women wore gold ribbons on their clothing. They held parades and marches to make men aware that women were being treated terribly.

In 1920 women finally won the right to vote.

32 USA
VOTES

SUSAN B. ANTHONY

- *She led the struggle to give women equal rights, including the right to vote.*

About half of the people in America are women, so it is hard to believe that at one time, women were treated very badly. In most places they could not own property. They could not become doctors or lawyers, and the jobs they did have paid much less than a man got for the same work. They had very few rights and could not vote. Susan B. Anthony wanted to change that.

Susan was born in Massachusetts in 1820 and raised in a Quaker family. Her parents taught her that ALL people were equal—both men and women. They also taught her that slavery was very wrong, so Susan decided to work for equality for all people.

GIVE MOTHER THE VOTE
WE NEED IT

VOTES FOR OUR MOTHERS

OUR FOOD   OUR HEALTH   OUR PLAY
OUR HOMES OUR SCHOOLS OUR WORK
ARE   RULED   BY   MEN'S   VOTES

Isn't it a funny thing
That Father cannot see
Why Mother ought to have a vote
On how these things should be?

THINK IT OVER

Susan began to go to public meetings and soon was speaking out about the evils of slavery. In 1852 Susan met Elizabeth Cady Stanton. The two women decided that it was also important to work for women's rights.

VOTES OR JAIL

In 1869, with slavery ended, it was time to do something about the way women were treated. Susan began a newspaper about getting women the vote. On Election Day in 1872, she decided to break the law. She tried to vote! She was arrested, put on trial, and found guilty, but she could not even speak in court because she was a woman.

NEVER GIVE UP!

For 45 years Susan traveled across America by stage coach, train, wagon, and on foot. She gave almost 100 speeches a year. Sadly, she died before women could finally vote in all the states.

In 1920, after a 70-year fight, a law was passed that gave women that right to vote. If Susan B. Anthony were still alive, she would be proud to see women who not only can vote, but who are helping to run the country.

Words To Know
- **Suffrage**
  (SUF-rij)
  The right to vote in an election.

In 1979 the American government honored Susan B. Anthony by issuing a $1 coin with her face on it. She was the first woman ever to be honored with a coin in America.

HELEN KELLER

- *She overcame disabilities and worked to help others who were blind and deaf.*

When Helen Keller was born in Alabama in June of 1880, she was a healthy baby, but all that changed when she was 19 months old. She got very sick and almost died. When she felt better, her mom realized that Helen could not see or hear.

Imagine a world where it is always as dark as the darkest night —a world with no music, no voices, no sounds. That was little Helen's world. She could not even talk because we learn to speak by hearing.

Helen became very angry. She had tantrums and screamed all the time. Her parents did not know what to do! By the time Helen was six years old, her parents were ready to send her away.

Then Helen's mom read a story about a blind and deaf child who had learned how to talk, so she took Helen to Baltimore, Maryland, to meet the man who taught the blind. His name was Alexander Graham Bell—the man who invented the telephone. He knew someone who could help.

Helen used the senses she had—smell, taste, and touch, to help her learn. She said she did not mind being blind but hated not being able to hear.

Words To Know

- **Disability**
   (DIS-a-bill-a-tee)
   A part of a person's body that does not work right and can make it hard to get things done.

That person was a teacher named Anne Sullivan. Anne had once been almost blind herself, but two operations helped her to see better. Anne came to Helen's house and got to work. She brought Helen a doll and spelled the letters D-O-L-L in Helen's hand, but Helen still could not understand.

Helen and Anne fought a lot at first—about brushing hair, getting dressed, even using table manners. Helen would only eat with her hands!

THE MIRACLE WORKER

One day Anne took Helen to the water pump where the Kellers got their water. Anne ran the cool water over Helen's hand and kept spelling W-A-T-E-R in her other palm, over and over. Finally Helen understood! All the anger left her. Within 30 minutes she had learned 30 words.

DOING THE IMPOSSIBLE

Even though Helen could not see or hear, she had a sharp mind and learned quickly. Soon Helen could read Braille *(Brayl)* books. Braille is an alphabet of raised dots. Each group of six dots represents a letter. Helen read a lot and became the first deaf and blind person to go to college. Anne sat next to her in class, spelling words into Helen's hand. In the years to come, Helen became famous. She wrote books and traveled all over the world. Helen Keller proved that having a **disability** did not mean that a person was useless. She fought for the rights of *all* people and proved that every life has value.

Anne Sullivan spelled words in Helen's palm. Try to write a word in someone's hand and see if he or she knows what word you spelled. It is hard!

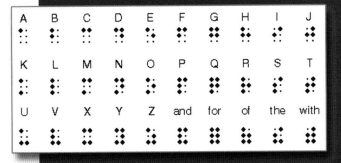

Helen learned Braille. Each Braille letter is part of a six-dot grid. Compare the A, B, and C, and you will begin to understand how it works.

When Helen grew up, she became very famous. She used her fame to make people aware of many issues, from helping people with disabilities to making sure women could vote.

Helen Keller is on the Alabama 25¢ piece from the U.S. state quarter series. Can you see her name in Braille?

ALABAMA 1819

HELEN KELLER

SPIRIT of COURAGE

2003 E PLURIBUS UNUM

Up until 1947, African Americans were not allowed to play with white ball players. They had their own separate league.

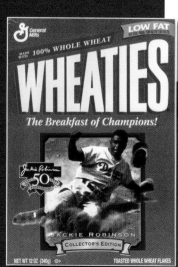

Branch Rickey, the manager of the Dodgers, knew that the Negro League had some of the finest ball players around. He wanted the best for his team, so he asked Jackie to come play.

In time, Jackie became a hero—a symbol of hope for people of all races.

JACKIE
ROBINSON

• *He was the first African American player in the major leagues of baseball. His actions helped to bring about other opportunities for African Americans.*

Being the very first to do something is hard. When he walked onto New York's Ebbet's Field on April 15, 1947, Jackie Robinson became the first person to cross a make-believe barrier called the "color line." This great athlete was about to make history as the first African American to **integrate** the sport that had become a symbol of America.

Jackie was born in Georgia in 1919. His family moved to California a year later.

Some people did not like the idea of athletes of color playing on white teams. Jackie got death threats. People cursed and spat on him. Pitchers tried to hit him with their pitches. Jackie stayed calm, held his head high, and kept on playing the best ball he could.

NO MORE!

Still, after a few years of insults—of unfair umpires' calls and hotels that would not let him stay with his teamates—Jackie decided to speak up about the way people of color were treated. Because he was such an amazing person, people began to listen to what he said.

For ten years Jackie played his heart out. He played in six World Series, but we remember him for much more. "A life is not important," he said, "except in the impact it has on other lives." Jackie Robinson, grandson of a slave and son of a sharecropper, led the way so that other African Americans could be treated as equals.

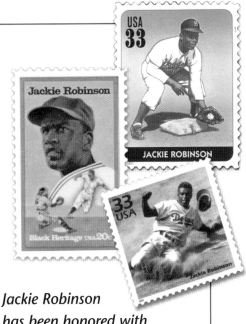

Jackie Robinson has been honored with several postage stamps. Schools and highways have also been named in his honor.

Words To Know
- **Integrate**
(in-tuh-GRATE)
To mix a racial or religious group into a community.

Jackie was a great hitter, a fast runner, and a quick fielder. After he left baseball, he became active in politics and worked hard to see that all people are treated as equals.

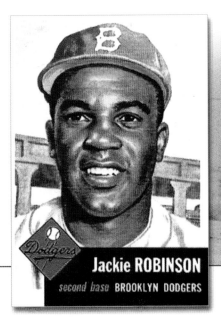

Jackie ROBINSON
second base BROOKLYN DODGERS

Martin Luther King hoped for an America where people would be judged by the goodness in their hearts, not the color of their skin. His dream is coming true.

MARTIN LUTHER
KING, JR.

- *He was an African American minister who worked so that all people would be treated fairly. He led peaceful marches and gave speeches.*

What if people decided that all folks with blue eyes were not as good as people with green eyes? What if someone told you that because you had freckles, you could not go to the movies? That would not be fair, but that is what happened to African Americans simply because they had dark skin. For many years they had to go to separate schools, ride at the back of the bus, and stand in some restaurants. Dr. Martin Luther King wanted to change that.

Dr. King was born in 1929 in Atlanta, Georgia. He grew up to be a minister, and when he spoke, folks listened!

The Fight for Civil Rights

A man from India had a great influence on Dr. King. Mahatma Gandhi used peaceful ways to get English rulers to leave his country.

In 1955 Rosa Parks was told to give her seat up to a white man on her bus ride home from work. She had been planning for this moment for some time. When she refused to get up, the police arrested her. Dr. King used her act to make people realize that unfair laws *had* to end.

Dr. King did not fight with fists or guns. He fought with words and peaceful actions. He asked other African Americans to join him in his cause. He and his friends told everyone to stay away from stores where the owners were mean to people of color. Dr. King told folks to have **sit-ins** at the restaurants and movie theaters where African Americans could not eat or see a film.

PEACEFUL MARCHES

Soon people all over the South started protesting. In 1963 Dr. King and his supporters led a huge march in Birmingham, Alabama, a city that had been treating African Americans badly. Dr. King led another huge march to Washington, D.C., and hundreds of thousands of people came. He spoke so beautifully that people wept. In 1964, thanks to Dr. King's hard work and his many **marches** and **speeches**, a new law was passed that ended **discrimination** because of color, race, place of birth, or religion.

Sadly, the law did not end discrimination, but it did make it illegal (against the law).

Martin Luther King stood on the steps of the Lincoln Memorial and said, "I have a dream." It became one of the most famous speeches ever!

Words To Know

- **Discrimination**
(dis-CRIM-a-nay-shun)
Treating people badly because of the color of their skin or the place from which they come.

- **Sit-in**
Refusing to move from a building, doorway, or seat to bring about change.

In 1963 Dr. King led hundreds of thousands of people to Washington, D.C., to try to change the laws.

Dr. King won the Nobel Peace Prize in 1964 for all his hard work. It is a very important award.

Sadly, Dr. King was shot and killed in 1968. We honor him by celebrating Martin Luther King, Jr. Day every January.

REV MARTIN LUTHER KING, JR.
1929 — 1968
"Free at last, Free at last.
Thank God Almighty
I'm Free at last."

AMERICA, LAND OF DIVERSITY

These five children have come to America from all over the world—from Asia, Africa, Europe, and South America.

• *The United States is a land of people with diverse ethnic origins, customs, and traditions.*

Imagine a big bowl. Now throw in lettuce and carrots. Toss in chicken and peppers. Top it with a tasty dressing. The carrots still look like carrots, but mixed with all the other flavors, they taste different. This colorful salad tastes yummy. America is a lot like that salad. There are people from all over the world living here. They have brought their **customs**—the beliefs and habits of the place from which they came. These ideas have all been thrown into the same "bowl" and "tossed" together.

All-American Things From Other Lands...

Pizza, bagels, tacos, cookies, ice cream, and a lot of our favorite foods come from other countries.

Soccer was first played in ancient China. Baseball began as an English game. Football started in ancient Rome. Many of our sports come from across the oceans.

No matter from where you and your family have come, you have something special to share—your **culture**. Culture is a mix of all the ideas, foods, and celebrations that are important to your family.

These girls are ready for Cinco de Mayo, a Mexican Holiday.

OLD WAYS, NEW WAYS

Many of the **traditions**—old customs—that people brought from other lands have become all-American favorites. It happened with Christmas trees (from Germany), Halloween (from Scotland and Ireland), karate (from Japan), and many more.

Americans have tried these new ways of doing things and liked them!

Some of our favorite games, such as *Go Fish!*, checkers, dominos—even hopscotch—came from far away!

Today's pop music, from hip-hop to hard rock to jazz, has its roots in Africa.

Holiday celebrations borrow from a lot of different customs. These people are celebrating *Kwanzaa*.

Words To Know

- **Citizen**

  (SIT-eh-zinz)
  Someone who by birth or choice is a member of a nation.

GOOD CITIZENS

- *People contribute to their community by practicing the responsibilities of good citizens.*

Do you treat everyone with respect? Are you careful with other people's things? Do you always tell the truth? Are you a good friend? Do you pitch in when someone needs a little help? Good for you! You are a good citizen.

Police officers, firefighters, doctors, architects, teachers, builders, and chefs are just a few of the people who help make communities strong.

Buckle up. It's the law!

What if everyone drove too fast or ignored STOP signs? People would get hurt. What if people took things that did not belong to them? A good citizen obeys the laws of the community, the school, and the classroom.

THE RIGHT THING

Suppose a firefighter takes a firetruck to a mechanic and the mechanic does a bad job fixing it. What will happen the next time a fire alarm sounds? What if the truck will not start? It is always important to do your best. A good citizen is **trustworthy**.

BY MYSELF!

Self-discipline *(DIS-a-plin)* and **self-reliance** *(re-LIE-inse)* are also important. People with self-discipline control their tempers when things do not go their way. They do not have tantrums or sulk. Folks who are self-reliant get things, such as chores, done without being nagged. A good citizen is also active in school and community, ready to help if something needs doing.

Our country has grown strong because we have always tried to share, be truthful, get things done for ourselves, and lend a helping hand to those who need it most.

A Good Citizen...

A good citizen respects the rights and property of others.

A good citizen helps out at school and in the community. Food drives, recycling, and raising money for the needy are just a few ways to help.

Good citizens are honest, trustworthy, and truthful, even if they might get in trouble for it.

We love America's holidays. On the 4th of July we celebrate Independence Day. On Memorial Day we remember fallen soldiers. On Veterans Day we honor people who fought in our nation's wars.

We pledge allegiance to our flag every day in school. We sing our national anthem at ball games and other big events.

Even though we call ourselves Americans, we still take pride in our "roots."

WE ARE ALL
AMERICANS

• *Americans are a people of diverse ethnic origins, customs, and traditions who are united as Americans by common principles and traditions.*

Americans may come from different ethnic groups and different countries, but we are united by something very special—the right to life, liberty, the pursuit of happiness, and equality under the law. That means that we must all have the same chances to learn, get jobs, and have a safe place to live, no matter from where we come. These rights cannot be taken away.

PLEASE COME TO AMERICA!

In our country's early days, we needed people to come and work here, but in the years that followed, some people were afraid of folks who looked or acted differently. They did not understand that diversity would be a good thing for the United States.

Our country made a lot of mistakes along the way—from slavery to not letting people from certain places come to America, but our government is trying its best to set things right.

Every year more than one million people move to America from other countries. Many are children your age. They might speak in a way that you cannot understand. They may wear head-coverings all the time or like spicy food, but they are boys and girls who love to laugh and sing and play—children just like you. They will learn to speak English and celebrate our nation's holidays. Many will grow up to become citizens and vote in our elections.

UNITED STATES

Our country is called the *United* States. We, its people, are also united, by dreams of building a land where folks of every color, of every religion, and from every land, can live happily and peacefully ever after.

Words To Know
- **Principles**
  (PRIN-suh-pulz)
  Basic values or beliefs that shape behavior and help us make good choices.

INDEX

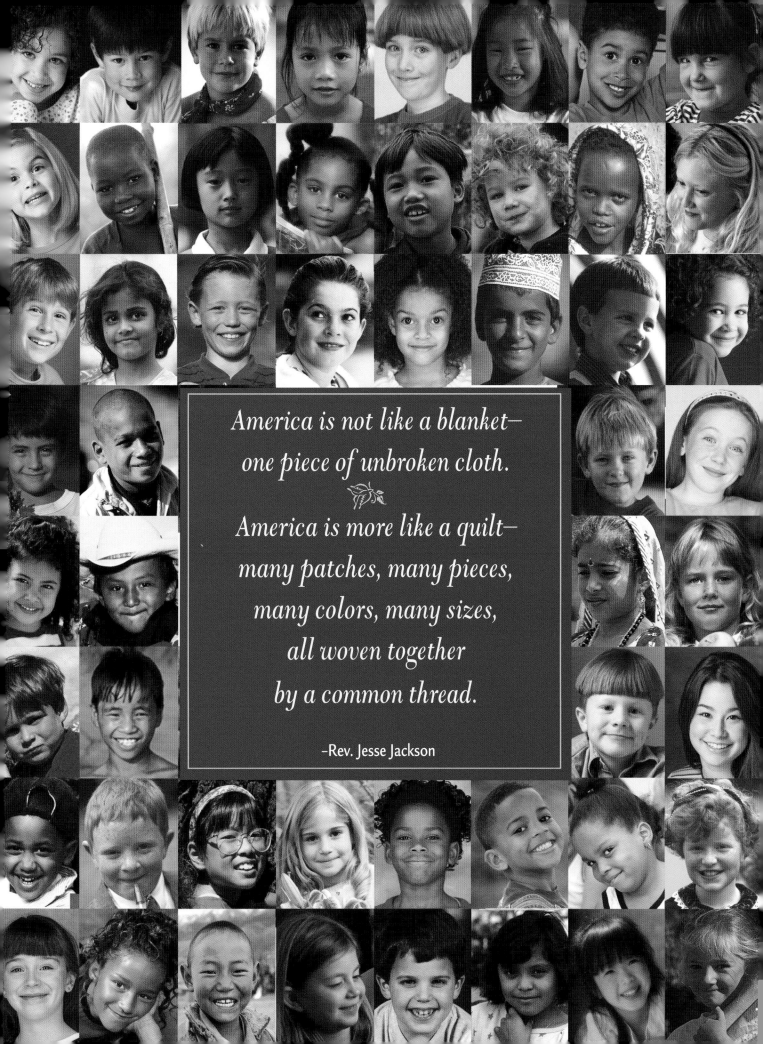

America is not like a blanket—
one piece of unbroken cloth.

America is more like a quilt—
many patches, many pieces,
many colors, many sizes,
all woven together
by a common thread.

-Rev. Jesse Jackson

RESOURCES

ADDITIONAL READING

Macaulay, David. *Pyramid.* Houghton Mifflin

Aliki. *Mummies Made in Egypt.* HarperTrophy

Fisher, Leonard Everett. *The Great Wall of China.* Aladdin Books

Benchley, Nathaniel. *Small Wolf.* HarperTrophy

Baylor, Byrd. *When Clay Sings.* MacMillan.

Mitchell, Margaree King. *Uncle Jed's Barbershop.* Scholastic Inc.

Fritz, Jean. *George Washington's Breakfast* Putnam Publishing Group

Fritz, Jean. *Just a Few Words, Mr. Lincoln.* Grosset & Dunlap

Golenbeck, Peter. *Teamates.* Harcourt Brace & Company

Dooley, Norah. *Everybody Cooks Rice.* Carolrhoda Books

ONLINE RESOURCES

www.ancient egypt.co.uk
An excellent site run by the British Museum.

http://www.webcorp.com/civilrights/martin.htm
Sound clips of Martin Luther King, Jr.

www.vahistorical.org
A wonderful source with lots of archival artwork to download for classroom display

www.nbp.org/ic/nbp/braille
The National Braille Press will send you free embossed braille alphabet cards for your class.

ACTIVTIES & ASSESSMENTS

A companion binder with 48 pages of classroom activities, reproducibles, graphic organizers, assessments and answer keys is available FREE with every 25-book classroom pack. Contact Five Ponds Press at www.fivepondspress.com for further information.

PHOTO CREDITS